Contents

We use **rocks** to make **buildings** and **walls**.

Rocks can be found on
the **beach**.

FIND OUT ABOUT

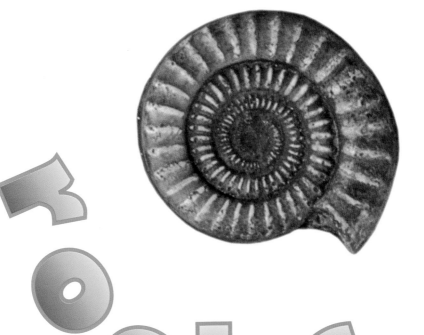

rocks

Terry Jennings

© **Terry Jennings / BBC Education 1996**

BBC Education
201 Wood Lane
London W12 7TS

ISBN 0 563 37468 3

Editor: Christina Digby
Designer: Jo Digby
Picture research: Emma Segal
Educational advisers: Samina Miller, Shelagh Scarborough
Photographer: Simon Pugh
Illustrator: Salvatore Tomaselli

With grateful thanks to: Elizabeth Cranney

Researched photographs: BBC Picture Archive (pages 4 bottom right, and 21 right); BBC/John Green (page 10 top); Britstock-IFA (page 14 top); Ecoscene (page 5); Frank Lane Picture Agency (pages 8, and 9 left); Terry Jennings (pages endpapers, 1 top, 4 top left, 4 top right, 12 top left, 12 bottom left, 21 left and 22 left); Natural History Museum (page 23); Robert Harding Picture Library (pages 9 right, and 19 left); Science Photo Library (page 4 bottom left); Sotheby's London, reproduced with kind permission (page 20); Still Pictures (page 15)

Origination by Goodfellow & Egan, Peterborough
Printed in Belgium by Proost

Where can we find rocks?

Our Earth is made of rocks. Often the rocks are covered by soil or water. But we can see rocks in many places.

The stones in the garden are pieces of rock. The pebbles on the beach are pieces of rock that have been worn smooth by the sea. The stones used to make many buildings are rocks.

In a city there are rocks. Many large buildings, roads and bridges are built with concrete made from rocks.

Rocks are dug out of **quarries**. They can be used to make **concrete**.

Granite is used for
some buildings,
roads and railways.

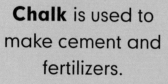

Chalk is used to
make cement and
fertilizers.

Sandstone is used
for building.

Thin sheets of **slate** are
used to cover roofs.

How many kinds of rock are there?

There are thousands of kinds of rock. Each kind of rock has a different colour and feel.

Granite is a very hard rock. It was made by a volcano.

Sandstone is made from tiny grains of sand. Long ago, these became stuck together deep under the ground and turned into rock.

Chalk is made from the shells of millions of tiny animals which once lived in the sea. When they died their shells were slowly squashed into chalk.

Marble can be used for floors, pillars, gravestones and statues. It can be black, white, pink, grey or mottled.

Obsidian looks like black glass.

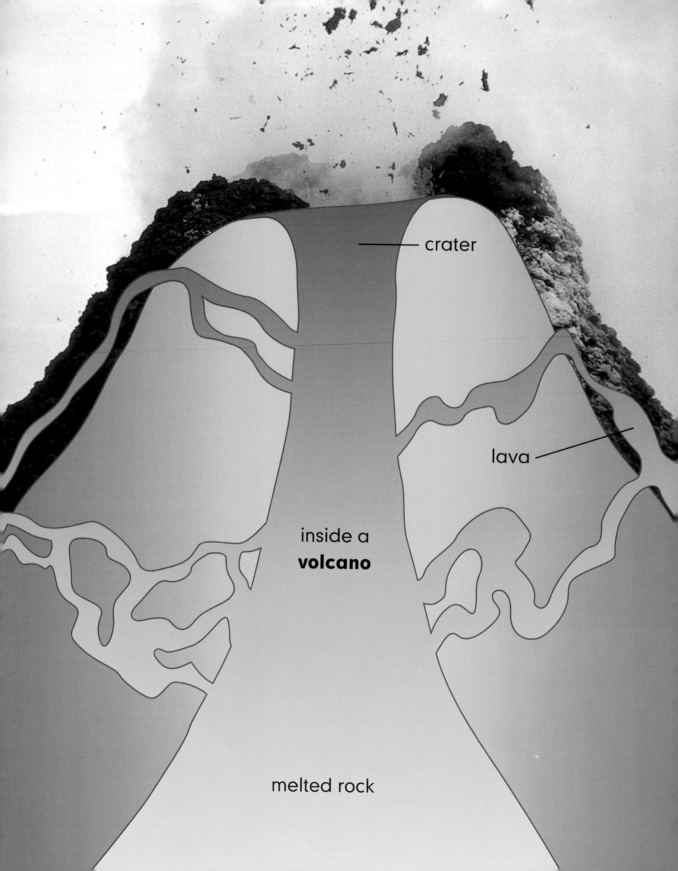

crater

lava

inside a
volcano

melted rock

Are all rocks hard?

Not all rocks are hard. Clay is a rock which is soft. Clay only goes hard when it is dried.

If any rock is heated very strongly, it turns soft and becomes runny. We say the rock has melted.

Deep inside the Earth it is so hot that the rocks have melted. They are runny like treacle. When a volcano erupts some of this melted rock, called lava, is thrown into the air.

People heat rocks until they melt to get metals from them.

When **lava** from a **volcano** cools it forms **new rocks**.

Some rocks can be **heated** to obtain **iron**.

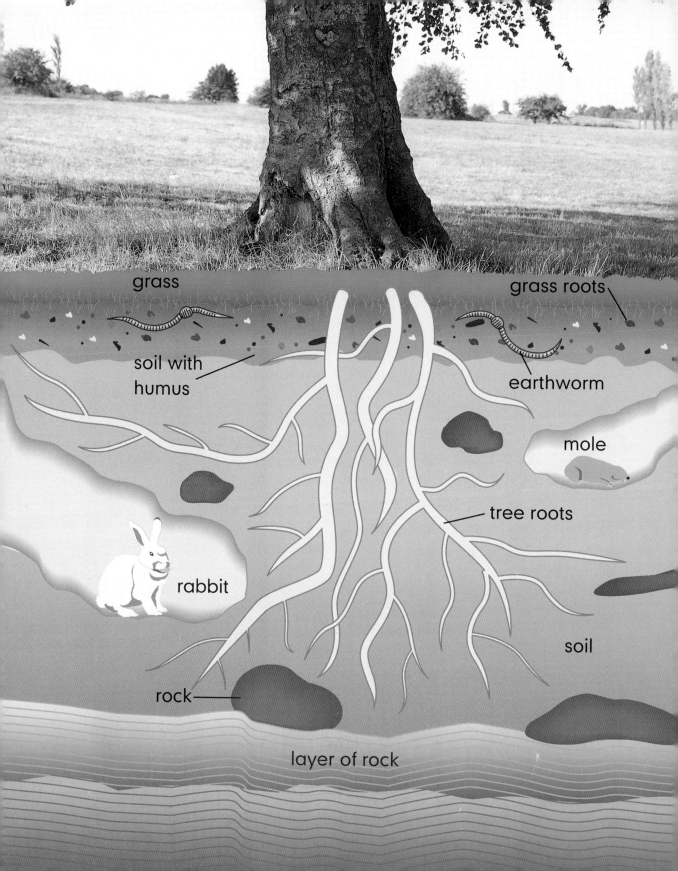

grass

grass roots

soil with humus

earthworm

mole

tree roots

rabbit

soil

rock

layer of rock

Is soil a rock?

Soil is not a rock, but it is made up of tiny pieces of rock. Soil contains water and air. It also contains the rotting parts of dead plants and animals. This is called humus.

Without soil, plants would have nowhere to grow. Without plants, humans and other animals would have nothing to eat.

See for yourself what soil is made of. Wearing gloves, put a handful of soil in a jar. Add water. Screw on the lid and shake the jar hard. Leave the jar overnight. Do not move it. Look at the layers in the jar the next day.

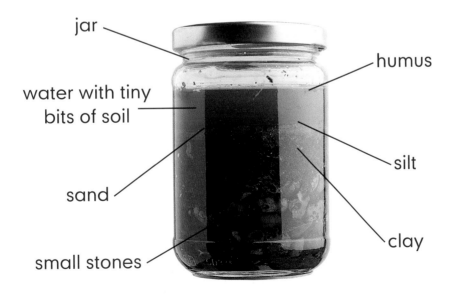

jar

humus

water with tiny bits of soil

silt

sand

clay

small stones

cliff

sand is made of tiny pieces of rock

boulder

pebbles

How is sand made?

Sand is made of tiny pieces of broken rock that came from larger rocks.

The wind and the waves help to break pieces off the cliffs by the sea. The pieces of rock fall into the sea. The waves bang them together, breaking them up into smaller and smaller pieces. After a long time the big pieces of rock have broken up into grains of sand.

This happens in a river too. The water in a river pushes some of the rocks together and small bits are broken off.

Different rocks make different types of sand.

People work in **mines** to dig **coal** out of the ground.

rock

lift

shaft

coal   tunnel

How do we use rocks?

For thousands of years, people have used rocks to build their houses.

Bricks and tiles are made from clay. Glass is made by melting limestone rock, sand and soda. Cement and concrete are made from rocks.

Coal, oil and gas come from rocks. Coal is made from rotted trees and other plants.

Oil and gas are made from tiny sea animals. When they died, the tiny animals sank to the bottom of the sea. The mud which covered them slowly turned into rock. The tiny sea animals became oil and gas.

blowing molten glass to make a vase

brick

mug

some things made from **clay**

flower pot

wall tiles

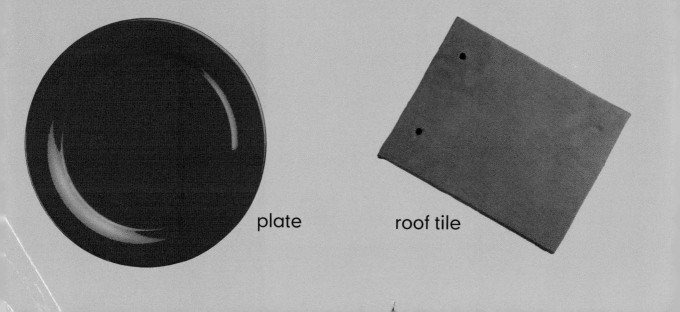

plate

roof tile

How do we use clay?

Clay is made of tiny pieces of rock much smaller than sand. They stick together well when the clay is wet.

Pottery, bricks and roof tiles are made from clay. The clay is dug out of large holes in the ground. The clay is shaped when wet. It is then heated in a kiln until it turns hard.

Dry clay powder mixed with limestone makes cement. Cement is mixed with water and sand to join bricks. It is also used to make concrete for buildings and roads.

wet clay being shaped on a potter's wheel

chalk in
toothpaste

metal in cutlery

pumice stone

some things made from **rocks**

sand in glass

lead pencils

sandpaper

How do we use rocks in the home?

Lots of things in your kitchen and bathroom are made from rocks. Everything made from metal comes from rocks. Things made of glass come from rocks. The tiles on the walls are made from clay, which is a rock.

Salt is a mineral. Most salt comes from mines underground. Pumice stone is a rock that was made by volcanoes. Talcum powder comes from a ground-up mineral called talc. Toothpaste contains ground-up chalk.

Salt can be found underground.

rock salt

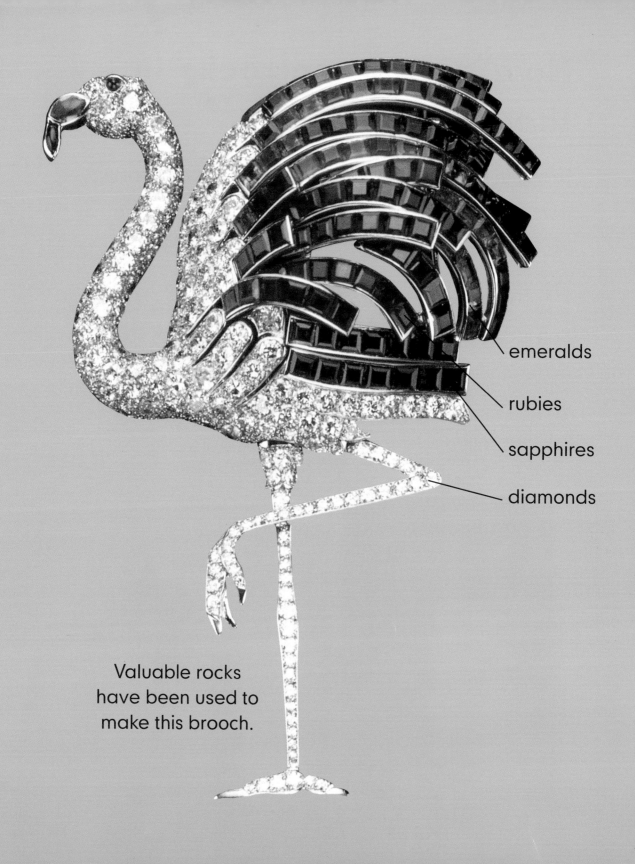

emeralds

rubies

sapphires

diamonds

Valuable rocks
have been used to
make this brooch.

What are the most valuable rocks?

All rocks contain minerals. Sometimes minerals form beautiful shapes called crystals. Crystals like rubies, emeralds and diamonds are rare and valuable.

The crystals are rough when they are dug out of the ground. They are cut and polished to make jewellery.

Metals are found in rocks called ores. Usually the ore is heated in huge ovens. The metal melts and runs out as a liquid. A few rocks contain tiny pieces of gold. The sand in some rivers also contains tiny grains of gold.

gold nugget

gold ring with diamond

uncut diamond

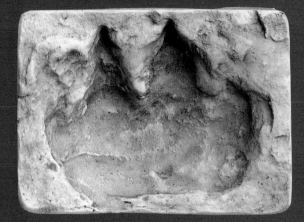

a fossil footprint

a fossil plant

a fossil seashell

a fossil sea animal

What are fossils?

Some rocks contain fossils. Fossils formed millions of years ago. When a plant or animal died, the soft parts rotted. The hard parts, such as the bones, shells and teeth, were buried under mud and sand. Slowly these parts turned into hard rock. The shapes and prints of the plants and animals are found in some rocks as fossils.

Because of fossils we know about plants and animals that lived long ago. We know that the first horses were the size of small dogs and that dinosaurs lived millions of years ago.

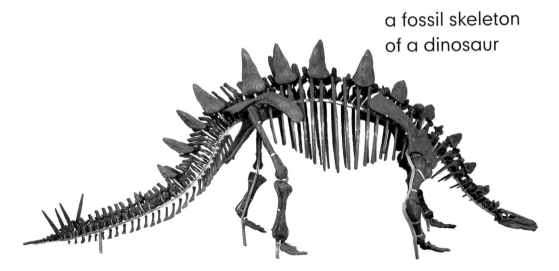

a fossil skeleton
of a dinosaur

Index

PRINTED IN BELGIUM BY

proost
INTERNATIONAL BOOK PRODUCTION